IMAGES
of England

NEWCASTLE
UNDER
LYME

Orme Girls' expedition to Chester during the Easter Term 1933.

IMAGES
of England

NEWCASTLE
UNDER
LYME

Compiled by
Delyth Enticott and Neil Collingwood

TEMPUS

First published 2000
Copyright © Newcastle under Lyme
Borough Council and Neil Collingwood, 2000

Tempus Publishing Limited
The Mill, Brimscombe Port,
Stroud, Gloucestershire, GL5 2QG

ISBN 0 7524 2074 7

Typesetting and origination by
Tempus Publishing Limited
Printed in Great Britain by
Midway Clark Printing, Wiltshire

Contents

Acknowledgements

The majority of images in this book are from the collection of Newcastle-under-Lyme Borough Museum and Art Gallery. This book has been produced in partnership between Newcastle-under-Lyme Borough Council and Tempus Publishing. The selection and research has been carried out by Delyth Enticott (Musuem and Arts Officer) and Neil Collingwood (local historian).

We would like to thank and acknowledge the following institutions and individuals for their assistance and kindness in the compilation of this collection of photographs: Staffordshire Arts and Museum Service (31, 36, 37, 38A, 38B, 39B, 40A, 52B, 59A, 76B), Newcastle-under-Lyme School (2, 80, 81A, 85B, 88B, 89, 90), Gregor Shufflebotham (42B, 64, 68A, 69B, 70B, 72, 81B, 102, 116, 117A, 128A), Miss L.M. Warham (6, 18B, 46B, 47, 55B, 57B, 83, 108B, 125B, 127A), Hugh Johnson (61), The William Colville Collection (21, 22, 23A, 25B, 26A, 30A, 41, 63B, 71, 98/99, 127B), Basil Jeuda (56B, 57B, 92, 93, 94B, 96A), Mr A.G. Ankers (35A, 103, 126B), The Warrilow Collection, Keele University Library (27A, 44A, 79A, 94A), Keith Meeson (56A, 57A,), Peter Christmas (109, 117A), Graham Bebbington (29B, 63A), Mr G. Burgess (34, 122B), Mr Boyce-Adams (120A), Mrs Hillary Ball (33), Mr Ron Whittaker (78A), Mr Martin Connop-Price, Mr P.B. Dyson (16B, 115, 121), Newcastle-under-Lyme Golf Club (43A), Mrs Storey (53B), Mrs Barker (32A), Mr Wilfred Spain (52A), Mr Shaw (67B), Newcastle-under-Lyme Library, Reference Section (18A), Mrs F. Hurley (53A, 69A), and Mrs J.E. Forster (60B)

In some instances the photographs lent to us were copies and we have made every effort of trace their original source but it has not always been possible to do so. If we have failed to acknowledge anyone in the production of this book then please accept our apologies. The responsibility of any omissions or error rests entirely with us. Any further information anyone might have about the images which appear in this book would be gratefully received.

Hospital Saturday Procession through Audley, *c.* 1910. Photograph by Thomas Warham.

Introduction

Since photographers first took up their cameras in Newcastle-under-Lyme in the 1850s, life in the town and borough has changed dramatically. Some of that change is clearly reflected in the selection of images presented here.

Since the twelfth century Newcastle-under-Lyme has held a regular market and was the most important town in the north of the county long before the city of Stoke-on-Trent came into being. The town became increasingly prosperous in the eighteenth and nineteenth centuries with the development of local industries such as coal and ironstone mining, iron-working, textile manufacture, and most importantly in the eighteenth century, hat making. These industries were assisted by improvements made in the transportation of their products, and the town was well supplied by both coaching, canal, and later railway links.

Most of the photographs in this book have not previously appeared in print. Many of the images have come from the Borough Museum and Art Gallery's own collection, but others have been kindly loaned or donated by other institutions, members of the public or private collectors.

Those people who are most often forgotten in works such as this are the photographers themselves. It is for this reason that the opening chapter of this book pays homage to those men (for men they invariably were) without whose effort, talent and pure inventiveness a book such as this could not possibly exist. They have provided us with enduring historical evidence, a resource which is constantly yielding new information. Whether the recording of a town, village or workplace was intended to serve as a lasting snapshot for the future is irrelevant, because even if it was not, that is what such images have become. We must take our hats off to Edwin, William and Wilfred Harrison, to Thomas Warham, William Parton and those others who have provided us with these fascinating studies. The sheer quality and skillful composition of their images often make them worthy of publication regardless of how mundane their subject matter. A high quality photograph of a shop window, taken purely in order to tempt the proprietor to part with money, may teach us about produce, display, fashions, prices, how employees were expected to dress and a multitude of other minutiae concerning the retail trade. To the generations who have grown up used to 'point-and-shoot' cameras, given the complexity and expense of taking and processing these early photographs it must come as a surprise to them that anyone ever persevered.

We also owe a great debt of gratitude to those who have held onto and treasured collections of photographs for many years. It is most gratifying that people are increasingly realising the importance and historical value of such collections.

The basis of selection was to choose images which would both have an instant impact but which also contained inherent historical detail. Every effort has been made in this book to present a broad spectrum of life in the borough, although it has not been possible to represent every village, occupation or important event inside its covers. It is in essence a mere taster of life in the borough over the last one hundred and forty years.

The obvious emphasis within these pages on certain families, schools or other institutions in the borough, and the absence of others does not imply any deliberate favouritism, it reflects only the existence of, and access to a good photographic record. Over a relatively short period during the compilation of the book, many new and wonderful photographs have come to light from a variety of sources; it is clear that there must be a great many more in private hands still awaiting discovery.

In previous publications, relatively little emphasis has been placed on rural aspects of the borough, the majority of which is still farmland. Indeed it is only about sixty-five years since the whole of areas like the Westlands and Clayton, now blanketed by housing, were populated mainly by cattle and sheep. It is to be hoped that the 'Country Life' section has gone some way towards redressing this balance, although photographs depicting rural subjects tend generally to be much harder to come by. One of the main intentions of this section is to provide a contrast between life in the town and that in the rural areas, but at the same time also to underline the symbiotic relationship between the two, a celebration of the diversity which is Newcastle-under-Lyme.

This selection of images has been compiled by two people, one who has spent more than forty years living in the borough and another who is a relative newcomer to the area. It is hoped that this may have led to the formulation of a book which is of interest both to natives and non-natives alike and that it is as interesting, enjoyable and stimulating to the reader as it has been to the compilers.

The Borough Museum and Art Gallery has a large photographic collection which represents the borough's recent history which is used as a resource for education and research. The museum would be interested to hear from anyone who would like to donate or loan images to the museum for copying. If any readers have additional information relating to any of the images used in this publication we would also like to hear from them.

Delyth Enticott and Neil Collingwood
Summer 2000

One
Early Photographs
and Photographers

Mayor Choosing ceremony, Market Cross by W. Parton. The newly elected Mayor of Newcastle-under-Lyme stands proudly in his regalia whilst the customary small boys pull faces from the Market Cross. In the background can be seen the sign for the town's museum, located in Lancaster Buildings from 1943-1954 before moving to its present location on the Brampton.

St Margaret's church, Wolstanton. This image, captured by Edwin Harrison around 1858, is one of the earliest known photographs taken in the borough, dateable because the church pictured here is not the Gilbert Scott Gothic revival building of 1858-1860 which stands there today, but its castellated predecessor.

East side of High Street before 1860. This is a vastly different scene today; next to the Castle Hotel is a timber-framed building long since demolished, and on the same side, a building stands where Hassell Street is today. The Guildhall arches remain open and the clock tower is not yet built. To the south stands the Weights and Measures Office, moved to Red Lion Square in 1877.

Edwin Harrison's studio, High Street, c. 1873. Edwin Harrison was Newcastle's most prolific and best remembered photographer. An artist, and the son of a gilder, he ran his photography studio in High Street until 1873. Here those premises stand empty awaiting demolition and the signs can clearly be read 'Removed to Liverpool Road'. After his death the family business was continued by his son William and grandson Wilfred, and survived for more than a century.

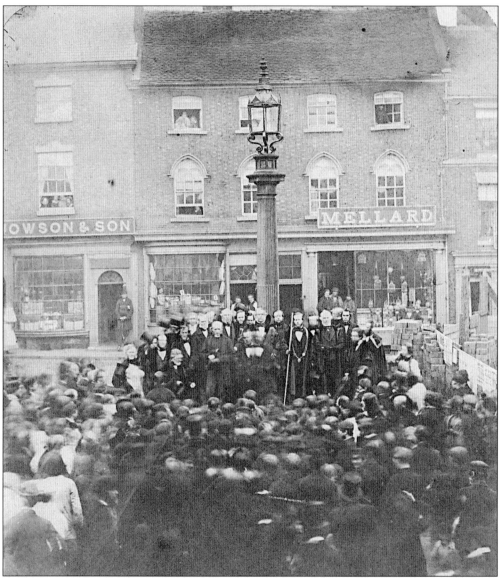

Mayor choosing ceremony, The Market Cross, *c.* 1860. This is another Harrison print, the hoarding and bricks at the end of the Guildhall suggest a date for this photograph of between 1860 and 1862. At this time the arches at the base of the building were being bricked up and the Clock Tower at the south end, paid for by J. Astley Hall, erected. This part of Newcastle appears markedly different today.

Harrison's studio, Liverpool Road. This photograph shows the house occupied by Edwin Harrison and his studio following his removal from High Street. Next to the house, behind the wall was a large well-kept garden where outside portraits could be taken. The identity of the man with the bicycle is not known but it seems likely that he was one of the family.

Interior of Harrison's studio. This advertisement for Harrison's studio was published *in 'A Graphic Description of Newcastle-under-Lyme'* in 1893. The studio was clearly purpose-built or at least adapted to benefit the photographers' art, with a large skylight, backdrops and 'props'. Also visible in the photograph is a book of samples and what might be either a 'magic lantern' or large plate camera.

View of Red Lion Square, *c.* 1875. For those who think that Wain's Chemists has been located next to St Giles' since the dawn of time, this view shows this not to have been the case. William Frederick Rimmel's grocery shop occupied the site during the 1870s and 1880s. Before

moving, Wain's was located just out of camera shot to the left. The cart to the left is in the livery of the North Staffordshire Railway.

Edward Prince of Wales at Trentham 1897. This Harrison photograph was probably taken in early 1897 when Edward Prince of Wales visited North Staffordshire and laid the foundation stone of the Sutherland Institute. The group, photographed outside the west entrance of Trentham Hall, also includes Cromartie, Duke of Sutherland, Millicent Duchess of Sutherland and Princess Victoria, granddaughter of Queen Victoria. The Prince is standing second from right.

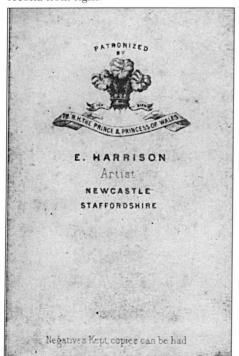

The back of a Harrison Print. The rear of this Edwin Harrison print states that he was patronised by their Royal Highnesses the Prince and Princess of Wales. How frequently this patronage was exercised is not known but the previous photograph is one example of it.

Cabinet card of a mayor, by E. Harrison
& Son (post 1873). This cabinet-card
was probably produced in the Harrisons'
Liverpool Road studio. The background
here is real although carefully arranged
for effect. In other studios, such as that
of Thomas Warham, items of furniture or
curtains were often skilfully painted onto
a backdrop.

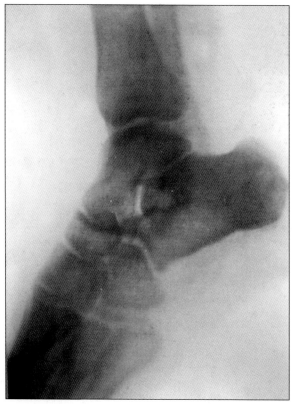

A Harrison X-ray. The discovery of
X-rays, and their use as a diagnostic
tool is attributed to Rontgen in
1895. Shortly afterwards the
Harrisons of Newcastle had
constructed their own X-ray
apparatus, now held in the Borough
Museum, and were producing images
such as the one shown here. This
print shows the foot of a woman
who had apparently stood on a pin.

Edwin Harrison's shop, Liverpool Road in the 1960s. The front of Harrison's Liverpool Road premises shortly before they were demolished in the 1960s to make way for the ring-road. Probably taken by Wilfred Harrison, a comparison of this photograph with the previous Liverpool Road image (see p. 13), shows how the family had altered the property to allow the development of a retail side to the business.

Thomas Warham's Studio, Audley, c. 1910. Audley was fortunate enough to have its own equivalent of Edwin Harrison in Thomas Warham, another artist turned photographer in the latter part of the nineteenth and early twentieth century. This is the purpose-built studio at the rear of Warham's house where he conducted his portrait sessions. The large skylights and walls of glass illuminated the elaborate backdrops which he often painted himself.

William Parton's shop and studio. After the Harrisons, the best known Newcastle town photographer is William Parton. Parton operated during different periods from both Hassell Street/High Street as shown here, and nearby Garden Street. His shop and studio opposite the Lamb Inn in High Street later became Bayley's Restaurant and the building still survives today although much altered on the ground floor.

Carte de visite by W. Parton, Garden Street. This *carte de visite* of an unknown sitter, was taken at the Garden Street Studio. The background has been 'dodged' out to concentrate attention on the subject. This differs from so-called Cabinet prints which were larger and ususally included a background.

19

From the **S**tudio of

W. Parton

9, Hassall's St
NEWCASTLE
STAFF.

COPIES MAY ALWAYS BE HAD
ENLARGEMENTS CAN BE MADE FROM THIS OR
ANY OTHER PHOTOGRAPH TO ANY SIZE &
FINISHED IN OIL, WATER COLOURS, OR CRAYON.

The rear of a Cabinet card by Parton. The reverse of *cartes de visite* and Cabinet cards were often so elaborately decorated, that the backs are sometimes considered more interesting than the photographs themselves! It was often on the reverse of these cards that a photographer's background as a conventional artist was revealed, as in this case where various hand-colouring techniques were offered.

The Clusters, Knutton by C.H. Deakin. Charles Deakin of 'Market Place' seems mainly to have produced postcards for private circulation rather than for a wider audience. His forte seems to have been photographing houses, with or without their occupants, but Deakin seems not to have been active in the area for long. The couple in the foreground of this picture, appear to have donned their Sunday best for the occasion.

Two

All About Town

The ironmarket, of which very few photographs exist, from Nelson Place around 1917, showing part of Marsh Street on the right. The trees on the right hand side are in the churchyard of St George's church which was greatly reduced when the ring road was laid. The Ebenezer Lecture Rooms and the small cottage which is now the Rose Bowl hairdressers can also be seen.(The William Colville Collection)

The Ironmarket (east) in 1930. This private house at the east-end of the Ironmarket was photographed from the Queen's Gardens just prior to its demolition in 1930. This elegant house, probably built in the late Georgian period, had extensive stabling, which is visible through the gates to the right of the property. The board erected outside reads '*Silverdale Equitable Industrial Co-operative Society Ltd - Site for new Emporium*'. The emporium building still stands today. (The William Colville Collection)

Proposed Co-op Emporium Site, *c.* 1930. It is interesting to note how even in the 1930s there were many domestic houses very close to the town centre. Today very few people live within the commercial centre of Newcastle. The land on which these buildings stood was reclaimed from a marsh in the late eighteenth century and were at that time on the very edge of town. (The William Colville Collection)

Marsh Street, 1930. The buildings on the left are the rear of the stables mentioned on the preceding page. Along with the house these were also demolished when the Emporium was erected. The Ebenezer Rooms on Merrial Street are to the right hand side of the picture. The demolition of houses and associated buildings in the town emphasises the pressure which existed to develop the commercial centre as a result of a large population growth in this period. (The William Colville Collection)

The Ironmarket, 1965. The Silverdale Equitable Industrial Co-operative Society Emporium is now built and the Municipal Hall is being demolished. It was replaced by the new library building. The library had been a part of the Municipal Hall from 1891-1958 when it moved to School Street.

Out with old and in with the new. This photograph, shot from the clock tower of the Municipal Hall during demolition in 1965, shows the new Civic Offices in Merrial Street nearing completion. The structure surrounded by scaffolding is a cleverly disguised chimney, similar to those of Charles Barry's on the Houses of Parliament. Also visible is Ryecroft School.

View from Ryecroft across Shoreditch, c. 1930s. It is possible to see the rear of the Ebenezer Lecture Rooms and the tower of the Municipal Hall. The posters in the foreground advertise features at The Savoy cinema in the High Street.

Looking west from the tower of the Municipal Hall, c. 1960. Showing the roofs of the Memorial baths on the right, the Roxy Cinema in the centre, and the roundabout before it was enlarged.

The borough treasurer's offices, Nelson Place, c. 1965. This impressive late Georgian building stood on the south side of Nelson Place and the photograph is easily datable as the Municipal Hall is undergoing demolition in the background. The bust of the Admiral Nelson which stands in the pediment of the building is now on display in the Borough Museum. (The William Colville Collection)

The ironmarket from Nelson Place, *c.* 1900. A much quieter scene then than it is today! Apart from the existence of a roundabout here today, the scene is still recognisable. The Municipal Hall has gone and Queen Victoria now stands on Station Walks although there are moves afoot to bring her back into the town centre. The pub on the corner was the Compasses, now the Crossways, which sold beer brewed by Ridgway's of Lower Street. This shot is unusual because it shows the beginning of Marsh Street on the right hand side of the picture, which has disappeared under the ring road. (The William Colville Collection)

Penkhull Street, *c.* 1927. A quiet afternoon in Newcastle town centre when what is now the High Street was the main thoroughfare through the town. This was taken before the access for vehicles to Hassell Street was made possible. The building to the left of what is now the NatWest Bank in the centre of the picture, was demolished around the time of the Second World War to provide a link to Hassell Street.

A flower seller outside the Guild Hall, 1910. It is likely that this photograph was taken following the death of Edward VII in May 1910 – the Union Jack on the Guild Hall is flying at half mast. A memorial service was held in the town on the Friday following his death. The absence of any female figures on this photograph may be significant because sometimes only men were allowed to attend memorial services while the women stayed at home!

'The Island Site' prior to demolition in the 1930s. This block was originally the Roebuck Coaching Inn owned by the Leveson-Gower's of Trentham Hall. As there was no room to expand the premises when it became politically expedient to do so, a new Roebuck was opened across the road where the Roebuck Shopping Centre now stands (see p. 65).

Red Lion Square 1897. The streets are decorated with bunting and flowers to celebrate the Diamond Jubilee of Queen Victoria. St Giles church in the background was redesigned and rebuilt by George Gilbert Scott in 1876 and replaced the Georgian church which was in a poor state of repair. The Weights and Measures Office on the right was moved to this location from the High Street in 1877 but was demolished in 1926.

The east side of Red Lion Square, c. 1958. The ornate building on the right is the Globe Commercial Hotel built in 1898 by Samuel Wilton in a similar style to the Municipal Hall. This replaced an earlier Georgian building. The whole of this block was demolished in 1968 to build the York Place shopping centre.

York Place, Red Lion Square, 1973. York Place Shopping Centre replaced the buildings on the preceding photograph and most of the south-western side of Merrial Street. The complex provided spaces for thirty-one new shops.

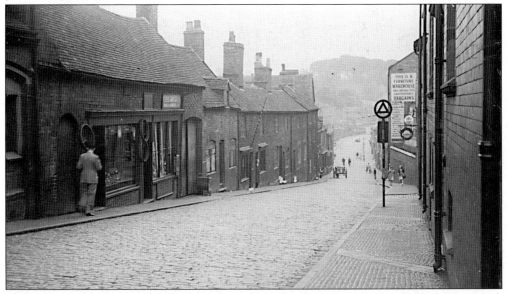

Friar's Street, 1937, showing the view down from the High Street towards Blackfriars Road, which is barely recognisable as the same view today. The shop on the far left was Spencer Collier's, a bicycle distributor. The furniture warehouse offering 'unrepeatable bargains' on the right was Carryer's. On the right, a small sign reads 'Taxi Sir?'. This marks the premises of William James Hubbard, Garage and Cars for Hire. Woolworth's and a multi-storey car park now stand on the left hand side leading down to a roundabout on the ring road.

Ball's Yard off Hassell Street in the 1930s. In stark contrast to the large houses in the Ironmarket and Nelson Place development, most of Newcastle's residents lived in small, cramped terraced housing in yards such as this. Soon after this photograph was taken families were moved to new council houses and the slums were demolished. (The William Colville Collection)

Newcastle from Clayton Fields. This shows how close the relationship between town and countryside was around the turn of the twentieth century. The Lyme valley in the middle ground is clearly still in agricultural use. Many major landmarks are visible in the distance – from left to right, St Giles' church and Holborn Paper Mill, the gasworks, The Guildhall, Municipal Hall, Holy Trinity Church and St George's church.

Three
Country Life

Four men singling mangolds in the fields of Keelehall's Home Farm in 1940, with Newcastle in the distance. The tower of St Giles' church is just visible on the left-hand side of the picture. Mangolds are a large turnip-type root vegetable grown as fodder for cattle and sheep. (McCann)

Cheney's or Seabridge Road Farm in Newcastle, *c.* 1890. Once part of the Butterton estate, it was occupied by Thomas Cheney in 1890. Once a working farm this is now a private home standing amongst newer houses on what is now Myott Avenue. This sixty-six acre farm was bought from the Miburn Swynnerton Pilkington family for redevelopment by Newcastle Corporation in 1921. The housing development built on the farm land was known as Seabridge Road Farm Estate.

The Downs family at The Hill Farm, *c.* 1910. The farm was on the land which is now part of The Westlands. The land was purchased by the Corporation from the Downs' in 1927 for redevelopment as the Hill Farm Estate. Newcastle developed and grew as a town between the wars and much farmland was lost to housing. In the decade between 1930-1940 a total of 6,453 houses were built in Newcastle!

The Hall Family at Hayes Farm, Butterton, in 1902; the family emigrated to Canada in the following year. At this time people were being encouraged to emigrate to alleviate poverty, and land in Canada was offered free to families (see page 70), so it is likely that the Halls took this opportunity. The farm was then taken over by Alfred Lea. From left to right: Grace, John, Percy, William, Mike, Nancy, Colin, Bob and Mary.

The Hall Family in Canada, c. 1908-1909. When the family arrived in Canada they were living in Saskatchewan and established a settlement there called Butterton. The contrast between the two family photographs is startling. From left to right: Percy, Grace, John, Mike, William, Elizabeth, Colin, Nancy, Bob. The dog went too!

A plough team at the rear of Highfields Avenue, May Bank, *c.* 1935. Wolstanton Colliery can be seen in the background. This photograph demonstrates the very close relationship which existed in Newcastle between domestic life, agriculture and heavy industry. Heavy horses moved at around $1\frac{1}{2}$ miles per hour and could plough about 1 acre per day.

Ploughing a field near the Wedgwood Monument at Butters Green, *c*. 1940s. The obelisk commemorates the life of John Wedgwood. Heir to his father's wealth from pottery and mining, Wedgwood was a rather eccentric character who lived the life of a country squire at his house in Bignall End. Prior to his death in 1839, he left instructions in his will to have the monument erected in his memory. The monument now stands a quarter of its original height having succumbed to a gale in 1976.

Red House Farm, Wolstanton. In 1861 the farm totalled 270 acres and was run by Henry Marsh. It was later farmed by the Forrester family until 1913. A trade directory of 1904 listed '*Mrs Caroline Forrester, farmer*' as the occupier. Purchased for development by Wolstanton Council in 1913, the farm had occupied land around what is now the Minton and Ellison Street area. A Kwik Save supermarket now stands near the site.

Horses cutting oats with a reaper binder at Maer Hall estate, 1937. These heavy horses are Percherons, a Lowland breed. They were introduced into Britain from Normandy following the First World War after displaying impressive strength in a military context. Horses like these

provided all the power needed on the pre-mechanized farm. They ploughed, drilled the seed, raked, turned and carted hay. Scenes like this could still be seen in the borough until the 1950s and 1960s. (McCann)

Miss Harrison standing outside a bull pen at Maer Hall, *c.* 1938. Miss Harrison was one of the two daughters of Mr Frederick Harrison, the shipping magnate who owned the estate. She is carrying an elaborate walking stick with an exotic animal head and an expensive camera. The daughters never married and after their deaths the Maer estate was sold by auction in 1964. At that time the Home Farm consisted of a farmhouse, and a multitude of buildings including a piggery range, a Dutch barn and a dairy building. (McCann)

Three gamekeepers probably taken at the Maer Hall estate, *c.* 1890. Rabbits and partridges hang from the gate. Gamekeepers were employed to ensure there was sufficient game such as pheasant and duck for the landowner to shoot. Their task was to eliminate pests and potential predators. Deterring poachers was another important function.

Frederick H. Burgess, implement and machinery merchant and agricultural engineer, c. 1940. This business was established in Newcastle around 1920. This warehouse was situated at No. 20 London Road, Newcastle, opposite the Holy Trinity church and supplied borough farmers with essential hardware. On display outside the store are ploughs, a roller and wheelbarrows.

Mr Bert Haywood, auctioneer, selling pigs at the Smithfield Cattle Market, Newcastle in the 1930s. The market was on land off Friars Street and was laid out there in 1871 at a cost of £1,200. The Smithfield replaced the animal market that had been held in the town centre since the medieval period. In the 1930s cattle and horse auctions were held by Messrs Haywood and Sons. The market closed in the early 1990s and is now the site of a Safeway supermarket. (McCann)

Maerfield Gate Farm, Maer in 1943. The farm is situated to the north of Maer village on the current A51 Newcastle to Woore road. (McCann)

Glass House Farm, Chesterton. The farm stood on the site of a seventeenth century glass works. The site was occupied in the late 1660s by John Beech of 'Glassehouse'.

Four
How the Other Half Lived

May Place, Brampton Road. This Victorian gothic house was originally the home of Harrison's, the ceramic colour merchants. It later became a children's home and was demolished in the 1970s to be replaced by a school, now a day-care centre of the same name. Parts of the original estate walls still survive today but the two lodges, one on Brampton Road and one in Sandy Lane have long since disappeared. (The William Colville Collection)

Dimsdale Hall, *c.* 1904. Unlike Whitmore or Bradwell Halls whose timber-framed structures were entirely encased in brick, the sixteenth-century Dimsdale Hall was given a Dutch-style brick frontage but the back was left exposed. Having fallen into disuse the timber-framed structure was demolished in 1904 leaving the frontage standing until the 1940s, as a reminder of its former glory. Today a small section of the original wattle and daub is displayed in a case in the Golf Club clubhouse.

Butterton Hall, *c.* 1914. This post-card shows the hall built by Sir William Pilkington at Butterton around 1840, although he never lived in it, preferring instead his estate at Chevet in Yorkshire. During the First World War the Hall was used by the military but like so many other large properties was subjected to severe damage. This postcard was sent by someone stationed there at the time. The Hall was demolished in 1924, leaving just the stable-block.

Newcastle Golf Club clubhouse, May 1962. The clubhouse at Newcastle Golf Club was originally built as a private house which owed its grandiose appearance to having been constructed from materials salvaged when Butterton Hall was demolished in 1924. Sadly, because the building was not really large enough to serve the Club's needs, recent extensions and alterations have now obscured much of the fine original stonework.

Bradwell Hall, c. 1920. Bradwell, formerly Bradwall Hall was the home of the Sneyd Family before their move to Keele. The original house was timber-framed but was later encased in brick. Due to the differences in architectural styles and scale, the floor levels of the original house bisect the later windows, meaning that first floor rooms have part of a window at floor level and part of a different window at ceiling height.

Watlands House, *c.* 1940. This photograph by Ernest Warrilow shows Lodge Grove, Porthill with Watlands House, the former home of Oliver, later Sir Oliver Lodge, and his parents, still standing in the background. The lodge which gave the Grove its name was demolished to make way for the present houses, but the mansion house itself survived until 1951.

Moreton House in the 1970s. Originally called Wolstanton Hall, Moreton House was built in the first half of the eighteenth century. Here the building stands empty and shows the ravages of time and mining subsidence. Unlike so many other houses in this state, Moreton House was saved from destruction by being dismantled brick by brick and the exterior used to face a new building erected a few metres away from the original site.

Moreton House. In another from the same series of photographs the large wing projecting from the rear of the house can be seen, together with the service buildings. The making of such a photographic record of a building prior to demolition is sadly all too rare but the three images here are from a larger set made when a decision had to be taken on what was to be done with the building.

Moreton House. An interior photograph taken at the same time as the previous image. In the corner can be seen a hand water-pump and trough probably dating from the mid-nineteenth century. The rot visible in the main ceiling beams gives a hint as to why the original structure was deemed beyond repair, and the drastic but laudable decision on its fate had to be taken. Sir Oliver Lodge conducted many of his scientific experiments here.

Whitmore Hall stables. Whitmore Hall is a timber-framed house which, in the late sixteenth century, was encased in brick to produce the handsome building visible. Trap-doors on inside walls of some rooms reveal original external timbers, showing how the house was enlarged. The beautiful stables pictured here still boast many of their original fittings.

This original print by Thomas Warham shows Audley Old Hall, a fine timber-framed building probably dating from the fifteenth century. Almost certainly built for one of the yeoman farmers of Audley, the Hall fell into disrepair in the early years of the twentieth century and was demolished in 1932. The porch bore the date 1230, perhaps indicating when a previous house on the site had been built.

Apedale Hall was built by Richard Edensor Heathcote of Longton Hall in 1826, following his purchase of the Manor of Apedale and commencement of extractive industry there. In this photograph the family on the steps are the Moseleys, including the young Sir Oswald, later infamous as leader of the British fascist 'Brown-shirt' movement.

A later view of Apedale Hall probably taken in the 1920s. How sad to think that in only a few years such a beautiful building would have fallen into disuse, fail to sell at auction and subsequently be demolished.

This atmospheric view shows 'Thistleberry Castle' in deepest winter. The 'castle' was a folly which stood behind the home of Joseph Mayer the antiquarian collector. No trace now remains of either the house, the 'castle' or its moat. It is a great pity that no-one seems to have photographed the house before it was replaced by the Thistleberry Hotel in the 1950s.

Five
Working Life

Butt Lane Industrial Co-operative Society, *c.* 1910. The members are seated outside the shop at the junction of Congleton Road and Church Street. The gentleman in the centre of the front row is probably the manager, James Culverhouse. The building is still in use by the Co-op as one of its chain of Late Shops.

A milk delivery from the company of Francis S. Butters, Dairyman of Hassell Street, Newcastle, around 1900. The gentleman on the cart has his milk churn and pitchers. Customers would bring their jugs to the door and the dairyman would ladle out the milk from the churn. These types of deliveries continued until the 1930s when bottled milk became the norm. This was photographed by Samuel Matthews, a photographer who had premises at 8 Merriall Street around 1904.

Hubanks' delivery vans 1940s. Delivery men unload a vehicle, piled high with fresh fruit and vegetables for Hubanks' greengrocer's in Hickman Street. It is unlikely that such a laden vehicle would be permitted on today's roads! In the 1930s William Hubanks had two greengrocer shops in Newcastle in Bridge Street and the Ironmarket, and a shop in Market Drayton.

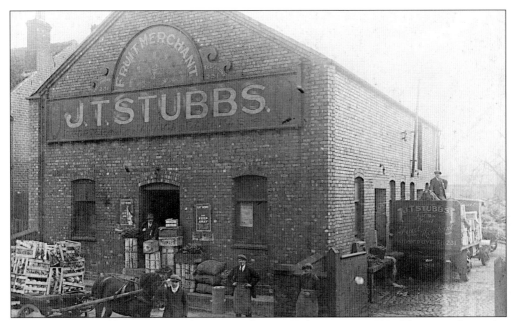

John Thomas Stubbs' Fruit merchant's warehouse, Kidsgrove, *c.* 1930. The sign above the warehouse door reads 'Importer of Jamaica Bananas'. This was located on Liverpool Road. In the 1930s he owned two greengrocery shops in Market Street. The figure in the doorway is presumably Mr Stubbs himself. The posters either side of the doorway read 'Eat More Fruit and Keep Away Flu' – sound advice! Mr Stubbs seems to have prided himself on his bananas which were eaten widely in this country from the 1920s (see p. 100).

Newcastle-under-Lyme postal workers including clerks and delivery men, 23 December 1915. The number of workers had greatly diminished as this photograph was taken after the rest had joined up to serve in the First World War. Considering the ages of some of the men on the photograph it is likely that more followed suit later. The gentleman in the centre on the front row is Stephen Henry Capon who was the borough postmaster.

Bickley's Tool Shop, Liverpool Road in the 1960s. This shows an immaculately turned out Wilfred Spain serving behind the counter at the well-stocked shop. When the Liverpool Road properties were demolished and the shop moved to new premises, but like many other tool and ironmonger's shops it finally closed its doors in the 1990s. Mr Spain, who became the proprietor, remained at work there until the last day of business.

Newcastle workhouse staff in the 1920s. The workhouse on Keele Road was built in 1838-1839 and replaced one on the Higherland. The workhouse was a last resort for those who had fallen on hard times, and provided shelter, food and medical assistance. Newcastle's workhouse could accommodate 350 paupers. The staff would have included a master and matron, school mistress/master, a medical officer, nurses, porters and a cook. It was demolished in 1938.

Cyril Bayley at work in the print shop of Bayley Bros, No. 42 High Street, Newcastle. Bayley's was a well-known family printing firm which had been in business in the town since at least 1867. They were printers, stationers, book-binders and auctioneers. (see p. 69).

Sarah Jane (Jinny) Amphlett was a domestic servant in Wolstanton in the late 1890s. As a maid Sarah would have been responsible for cooking, cleaning, laundry and shopping. Most working class homes would have one or more members of the family in service. Domestic service provided much employment in Newcastle in the Victorian period as most lower-middle class families would have had at least one servant.

The cutting room at Enderley Mills, Newcastle, c. 1916. The mill opened in 1881 specialising in the manufacture of uniforms. At this time the mill was owned by Messrs J. Hammond & Co Ltd. and specialised in police, army and railway clothing.

Enderley Mills elaborately decorated to celebrate the end of the First World War in 1918. The worktables here are piled high with army uniforms made to fit men destined for the front line. Happily the uniforms seen here were surplus to requirements.

Wheatley's Tileries, Trent Vale in the 1930s. This image shows workers mixing materials tipped from trucks pulled by the miniature diesel locomotive shown. Wheatley's survived into the 1980s and although the site is now a retail development, its large, water-filled marl hole still remains.

Miners take a break and pause for a photograph at Diglake Colliery, Audley, c. 1900. Coal had been mined in the area since at least the thirteenth century. During the eighteenth, nineteenth and most of the twentieth century, mining was the largest employer in the district.

In Loving Remembrance of
THE UNFORTUNATE MINERS,

Who accidently met their death by the Flooding of the Diglake Colliery, Audley, North Staffordshire, January 14th, 1895.

Death did to us short warning give,
Therefore, be careful how you live ;
Make nothing strange, death happens unto all
Our lot to-day—to-morrow you may fall.

In health and strength they left their homes.
Not thinking death was near :
It pleased the Lord to bid them come
And in his presence to appear.

When we arose at early morning,
Full of health, all blithe and gay,
We little thought it was the dawning,
Of our last and dying day.

Short was their lives in this vain world,
And sudden was their death,
A moment speaking to their friends,
The next they lost their breath.

" NOT OUR WILL, BUT THINE O LORD, BE DONE."

A Remembrance Card for the Diglake Colliery disaster of 1895. There were two hundred and sixty men and boys in the Diglake mine when it was inundated by water. Seventy-eight perished in the disaster. Only three bodies were ever recovered.

Talke-o'the Hill. A rare underground photograph of a miner at the seam at Talke-o'the Hill pit in the early twentieth century. Note the lack of protective clothing worn by the miner in the days before health and safety was a priority. The last deep coal mine in the borough closed at Silverdale in December 1998.

The Mines Rescue Team at Holditch Colliery, waiting to descend in the cage after the disaster on 2 July 1937. Thirty men died and eight were injured owing to fumes and two explosions. A fire had started on the face at about 6am followed by a series of small explosions and the rescue team went down at 7.30am. At 10am, while the team were still underground, another explosion occurred which killed twenty-seven men. The team is wearing breathing apparatus.

Jamage pit ponies after being rescued from the mine at Talke. Two underground explosions occurred on 25 November 1911. The first killed six men and was caused by the afterdamp. There were no men in the mine when the second explosion happened but twenty-seven ponies were killed as a result of the explosion. These emaciated ponies had spent twenty-two days trapped underground before being rescued.

In the pumping house at Silverdale Colliery, *c.* 1900. The pump was used to remove water from the deep excavations – a matter of life or death to the miners. The engine had possibly only just been installed, which could be the reason why this photograph was taken.

Whitfield Colliery Prize Band, winners of the Silver Challenge Cup at Audley in 1924.

Miners with a pit pony at Nabbs Wood
Colliery during the national strike of 1926.
The strike was caused by the miners being
threatened with reduced wages and increased
hours. The general strike lasted eight days but
the miners battled for seven months leaving
many families impoverished.

Sergeant Hambleton , a Newcastle fireman in 1894. The fire brigade was a voluntary force at this time. Mr Hambleton worked for the gas committee and fell to his death from the clock tower of the Municipal Hall, whilst working on the gas lights which illuminated the clock, on 22 May 1897. This Cabinet card of him belonged to a fireman, Mr Arthur Ernest Pointon, who was probably given the card as a memento after his colleague's death.

Fire-fighters of the Auxiliary Fire Service tackling a blaze at Chesterton during the Second World War. Chesterton was the victim of the worst bombing raid of the war, in North Staffordshire, on 16 December 1940, when fourteen people were killed and sixteen injured.

Six
Shops and Shopping

Herbert Henry Steele's Butchers, London Road, Chesterton, c. 1910. Wheat's newsagents is next door. The gentleman in the doorway is presumably Mr Steele himself who probably paid a local photographer to produce a small number of prints of his shop. Hygiene standards, which did not change significantly until the middle of the last century, were clearly less stringent than they are today.

The Stones, c. 1895. For centuries Newcastle hosted the most important market in North Staffordshire. This view, before the coming of the trams in 1900, shows traders selling their wares from carts or rickety stalls. The reason for the market acquiring the name 'The Stones' is apparent from the foreground. Newcastle's main street was deliberately constructed especially wide to accommodate the market.

The Ironmarket, in the 1890s. Another general view of shops and shopping, this time in the Ironmarket. Examination of such scenes through a lens reveals a wealth of details such as shop names, wares and even prices. By using shop names in conjunction with trade directories, rate-books and census returns, it can be possible to date pictures like this one to within a few months.

Collier's Tobacconists, Friar's Street, *c. 1937*. Alfred Collier's Tobacconists shop, situated at No. 3 Friars Street. This rare photograph also shows the rear entrance to Woolworth's. Both Woolworth's itself on Penkhull Street and the shops and houses along Friars Street were timber-framed buildings, demolished in the 1940s and 1950s.

George Taylor and Sons, plumber and decorator, Marsh Street. The whole of Marsh Street has now disappeared under the dual carriageway between Nelson Place and Liverpool Road, making this photograph of Taylor's shop, complete with horse, cart and probably Mr Taylor himself, an unusual and interesting item. The business was in existence for at least twenty-eight years between 1900 and 1928. (The William Colville Collection)

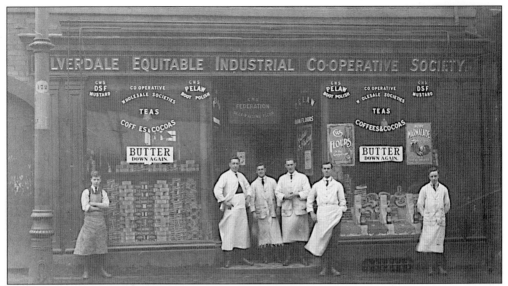

Silverdale Equitable Industrial Co-operative Society. This photograph of the staff outside the shop was apparently taken on 17 May 1923. Window advertisements features the Co-op's (CWS) own brand products such as Pelaw Boot Polish and DSF mustard. This shop was possibly on London Road, Newcastle, or may have been in an outlying district of the borough.

Mrs E. Wild's High Class Modiste & Ladies Outfitter, Merrial Street, 1920s. The shop remained open until at least 1932 when the proprietor was listed as Mrs Janet Wild. It is difficult to imagine such an establishment surviving for more than a few weeks in Newcastle today. Fortunately, although the business is long gone, the terracotta decoration on the outside of the shop remains intact. This card was sent to Mrs E. Wild.

Lancaster Buildings, High Street, 1930s. Here an artist's impression of Lancaster Buildings has been superimposed onto a photograph of where the building was to stand. In the 1930s there was great controversy over what was to be done with this 'island site'; it is a pity that the decision was not deferred, so that the eighteenth century coaching inn which previously stood on the site could be saved (see p. 27).

Lancaster Buildings, High Street, 1930s. No longer just an artist's impression, Lancaster Buildings soon after its completion. The building remains virtually unchanged today, although the shop's tenants have changed many times. The photograph reveals the damage inflicted on Carryer's the Pawnbrokers by a fire which occured after the previous photograph had been taken.

William Hubank & Son, greengrocers and florists, 1930s. The High Street store prior to modernization, with produce being sold from trays supported on barrels. As advertised Hubanks also ran a second shop in Market Drayton at the time. The firm remains one of the oldest surviving businesses in Newcastle, still maintaining a shop in Merrial Street today, (see p. 50).

Hubanks, 1950s. The High Street Store again during construction of its 'ultra-modern' frontage in the 1950s. This appears almost complete, awaiting only the application of ceramic tiles or other finishing detail to the concrete surrounding the windows. Although the building still survives today, its former existence as a grand Georgian House, built in 1747 for John Bourne, is no longer immediately obvious.

Hubanks, in the 1950s. Inside the 1950s shop (see previous photograph), the barrels and trays have now been replaced by modern counters. The produce remains much the same, as does the way it was to be served by a large staff of counter-assistants, very different from today's supermarkets. The thin paper strips on the oranges read 'No Ration Books Required'.

Shaw's Fish and Chip Shop, Penkhull Street, late 1920s. Another Newcastle business with a long history, Shaw's chip-shop opened by Thomas Turner Shaw around 1920 in Penkhull Street, and remains a thriving business today. The posters in the window advertise the King's Theatre and the Pavilion Cinema, one of those belonging to Robert Beresford (see p.70).

Mannequin Parade at Co-operative Emporium, Ironmarket, 1932. This high quality photograph shows members of staff at the Co-operative Society Emporium dressed as for a wedding. The lady on the right is Marjorie Beasley, later to become Mrs Shufflebotham, aged eighteen, and second from left is Phyllis Horton. The Co-op staff were very active in such events as historical pageants, perhaps because they were so accustomed to dressing up at work.

Fred Cooper, 'Hokey-Pokey Man', 1930s. Fred Cooper grew up at Red Street, Chesterton and later moved to Bignall End. The precise location where this picture was taken is not known but as Fred was clearly quite young in the photo it may have been taken whilst he was living in Chesterton. It is interesting to speculate on how long Fred's ices might have remained saleable on a hot summer's day.

Bayley Brothers Printers, High Street. This 1920s picture shows the elaborate decoration, which fortunately still survives today, on the frontage of Bayley Bros stationery shop and printing works. High on the frontage is the monogram of the founder of the business, Thomas Bayley and Godwin's printers still operate from the rear of the premises, although it is no longer a family business, (see p. 53).

Maypole Dairy Co Ltd, High Street, c. 1910. A Maypole window display showing that aggressive advertising and price-wars are clearly nothing new. One display states that 'The Tremendous success of Maypole Tea has very much upset our rival competitors'. The remainder offers a free half-pound of margarine with each pound bought. It is easy to imagine the irritation caused to smaller retailers by the adoption of such tactics.

Chesterton Post Office, *c.* 1902. The entire window display is dedicated to promoting emigration. One hundred and sixty acre plots of farm-land in Western Canada are offered absolutely free, presumably during a period of economic hardship. Transatlantic passage was to be via Canadian Pacific Railway or Cunard Line vessels and samples of crops to be grown are displayed. The man on the step is probably the proprietor Gerald Greatrex, (see p. 33).

Beresford's Cycle Repair and Accessory shop, Merrial Street. Robert Beresford was a well-known businessman who ran several cinemas, including the 'Regal and Pavilion', later the 'Rex' and 'Rio' in Newcastle's High Street, a garage and several cycle repair shops. Beresford was elected Mayor of Newcastle in 1927, 1928 and 1929. The shop in the picture later became Brown's Cycles which continued operating into the 1960s.

Seven
Pleasures and Pastimes

Pat Collins's Motors Carousel at Newcastle Wakes, *c.* 1910. The Wakes fair was held in September of each year and carousels such as this would have been placed on 'The Stones'. These events brought a touch of magic and excitement to the town and the mill and mine workers were able to leave reality behind, if only for one day. These fairs were varied affairs. The Wakes of 1847 boasted Highland games, clowns, donkey races, tip-cat, drummers, fifers and 'Grin Though A Collar' – an opportunity for the townspeople to *'show their eminence in ugliness'*. (The William Colville Collection)

Historical pageant-goers in July 1931 dressed in medieval costume. The lady in the centre is Mrs Bird.

Workers of the millinery and mantles department of the Silverdale Equitable Industrial Co-operative Society Emporium in the 1930s. This shop was in the Ironmarket opposite the Queen's Gardens. They are dressed for the historical pageant of 1935 celebrating the anniversary of the Guild merchant charter.

The winners of a dancing competition being presented with their cups in 1954 by the Mayor Miss Ethel Shaw. The competition took place in the main function room of the Municipal Hall which was used for social events such as exhibitions, concerts and civic occasions. This event was sponsored by Hubanks' greengrocers.

VE Day celebrations outside the Coronation Cinema, Hall Street, Audley. The cinema opened in 1912. The proprietor was Mr Albert J. Plant. The cinema became a bingo hall in the 1960s and is now used and owned by Audley Players' Theatre Club. The proliferation of cinemas in small towns and villages is in marked contrast to todays emphasis on large multi-screen complexes.

The staff of the Grand Picture Palace, Congleton Road, Talke in 1935. The posters advertise a film called 'Her Sporting Chance – a thrilling drama' and Anita Stewart in 'In Old Kentucky – the grandest picture for years a super production'. Opened in the 1920s it was later renamed the Regent Cinema under the licensee and manager David Wilde.

An outing organized by Frank Proctor's Motor Garage of Bignall End in the 1920s. Proctor established his business around 1921 and it continued until around 1937. The garage itself was based at Raven's Lane.

A Sunday School treat in 1898, an outing to the rural Clayton Green, presumably for a picnic. A break from the crowded town would surely have been welcome. Although Clayton Green is built up today, in the late nineteenth century it was very rural and this demonstrates how near the centre of Newcastle was to the great outdoors. It was during this period that excursions became popular and were not confined just to the wealthier classes.

An indoor riding school, 1936. The school was part of the covered market building on Penkhull Street. The building was on three levels and the school occupied the lower level. Poor weather had prompted Mr Timmis, owner of Standon Bridge Riding School to seek an indoor venue, and he opened this school in Newcastle. The man on horseback on the far right, may well be Mr Timmis himself. The building was later used as a roller-skating rink called 'Rollerdromes Ltd' and a corporation garage. (McCann)

North Staffordshire Field Club in Maer Woods. This photograph was taken by Mr Thomas Pape during an excursion on 27 June 1927. The group were on a visit to the Iron Age Hill fort at Berth Hill. The Field Club was established in the 1860s, its members being interested in archaeology, history, botany, zoology, geology and photography amongst other things.

The Railway Inn, Chesterton, 1950s. Mrs Alice Mary Bettaney, Mr Ev Rhodes and others pictured outside the Railway Inn with the Audley and District Darts League shield which they had just won.

The official opening of the Whitfield Avenue Pavilion, c. 1938. Opened by the Mayor of Newcastle, Mr T.O. Harper, this community hall was built as part of the development of the Westlands Sports Ground to provide an amenity for public and private use. The pavilion was built by T.S. Hedley of Newcastle for £2,843. The pavilion has now been replaced by a brick building.

'The Mustangs' play at the Savoy in Newcastle, 1950s. 'The Mustangs' sang skiffle songs on Saturday mornings before the film. The amplifiers were converted radios and occasionally tuned into radio stations during the performance! The Savoy on the High Street was originally called The King's Hall Cinema and could accommodate an audience of over 1,000. Since the 1950s the building has been a cinema, a bingo club and is now a night-club called Rockin' Robin's. From left to right: Geoffrey Todd, Keith Meeson, Barry Thompson, Kenneth Card.

A group of happy people from Kidsgrove on a Festival of Britain outing in 1951, they have just been though the Harecastle Tunnel. The tunnel on the Trent and Mersey Canal was opened in 1777 and runs underground for over one and a half miles.

A cricket match on Wolstanton Marsh, *c.* 1890. What is particularly interesting about this image is that there are two female batsmen. It was probably a match held for a special event or for charity, as neither female batsmen nor top hats were customary at matches in this period!

A tug-of-war during a sports day at Beasley Fields, Chesterton, *c.* 1910.

Orme Girls' School tennis team, 1911. There was a great deal of emphasis on sport at the school. The heavy, modest and cumbersome outfits must have restricted movement and are a world away from what is worn today. Not all girls at the school were local, some came to Newcastle by train and others had lodgings in the town. From left to right: G. Daniel, M. Brown, M. Bagnall, C. Daniel, H. Bodley, M. Cowlishaw, E. Lewis, M. Bodley.

Orme Girls' School cricket team, 1920. When the school was founded in 1897 it did not have its own playing fields. As a consequence the girls used the boys' pitches at the High School and possibly used the cricket pitch through necessity rather than enlightenment. From left to right, standing: D. Stone, M. Wright, W. Wainwright, G. Allen, J. Goldstraw. Sitting: C. Hay, E. Abbott, I. Blaney, D. Dean, M. Nevitt.

Orme Boys' School football 1st XI, 1915-1916. The first Orme School was founded in the early eighteenth century through Revd Orme's endowment. In 1916 the school was based at the Higherland. The boys are sitting on the steps in the school-yard. From left to right, back row: J. Morrall, J. Hall, E. Maddock. Middle row: R.J. Hallen, W.G. Henshaw, C.H.S. Johnson. Front row: H.H. Broadgate, W.H. Fox, R. Warburton, S. Jenkinson, E. Hughes.

St George's Church Harriers, 1906-1907. This athletics team was established by the evangelical Revd Albert Baines who was responsible for increasing the congregation of the church and who established a temperance mission with an emphasis on activities such as crafts and sport. He was assisted on the sports side by his curate, Reginald Crabbe, who was both a Cambridge Blue and an Olympic athlete, and later became the Bishop of Mombassa. From left to right, back row: P. Bloor, J. Kite, J. Clowes. Middle row: J. Benton, N. Dalrymple, D. Doxsey, A. Mycock, S. Ford, Revd A. Baines (president), Revd R.P. Crabbe, C. Cliff, E. Hales, H. Wilkes, J. Machin. Front row: W. Boulton, W. Hulme, E. Glover, H. Martin (vice-captain), T. Smith (captain), E. Bishop (hon. sec.), S. Oliver, W. Doxsey. Sitting: B. Nind, G. Rowe, F. Martin.

Chesterton Football Club, early 1900s. They won the Sentinel Cup, Hanley and District Cup and were finalists in the Staffs Junior Charity Cup, and runners up for the Junior League Championship three years running. They won the Sentinel Cup without a goal being scored against them. From left to right, back row: ? Eadlington, E. Farrell, S. Flint, A. Sheldon. Middle row: J. Wright (secretary), D. Hogarth, G. Wood, ? Boullimier, W. Capper, H. Salmon. Back row: E. Pinner, W. Brindley, E. Rhead, W. Machin, S. Lawlor.

The Orme Football Club, 1950s. This team later developed into what is now Newcastle Town Football Club. The player third from right on the back row is Ken Stretch.

Eight
Schooldays

A class at Ravens Lane School, Audley, photographed by Thomas Warham. On the desk at the front is a holder bearing a number which clearly identifies which class is being photographed, and no doubt used to order reprints and to ensure that the correct negative was printed.

Friarswood Boys' standard 4 class. Some of the pupils depicted in this class photograph look rather as though they have just come up from a shift 'dine th' pit' rather than out of 'schoo'.

Chesterton Board School, 1895. These boys sit proudly holding slates on which their attendance records have been written. The star pupil had apparently never been absent since commencing at the school more than five years previously.

84

Silverdale Council Girls School, c. 1900. Although predominantly a mining area whose populace was unlikely to be very well off, this class of girls look surprisingly well-dressed, well-nourished and, for the most part, cheerful.

Orme Girls' prize-giving at the Municipal Hall, 1948. Like the Municipal Hall itself, prize-giving ceremonies are largely a thing of the past. This photograph is particularly interesting as despite so many people objecting to its demolition, no-one seems to have properly documented the interior of the 'Muni' before it was demolished, and very few images are known to exist.

Friarswood County Primary School, formerly the Newcastle British School. The school was built on land donated by the Duke of Sutherland and an inscription to that effect ran across the front of the school beneath the date-stone.

Mr ('Daddy') Dawson presiding over a reading session at Friarswood School in the 1960s. The blackboard states how 'Puss went out to find a castle for his Master'. It might be interesting to discover what children of the same age today would make of this rather surreal-sounding reading material!

The school hall, Friarswood. Children today would probably fail to find much difference between photographs of Friarswood School and descriptions of Dickens' Dotheboys Hall. Unlike the latter however, Friarswood School survived into the 1960s despite having been condemned many years earlier, due to structural damage.

Friarswood's headmasters office, c. 1960s. This office remained unchanged until the closure of the school. As can be inferred from the windows and skylight, the office was situated in a small square extension added to the side of the school. There is no sign of a radiator and with a bare tile floor the office must have been icy in winter.

A Friarswood School Attendance Certificate; this certificate was presented to Joseph Cheney for 100% attendance during 1926. It is redolent with images of King, Country and Empire and implies that regular attendance at school would lead to greater things.

The Orme Girls' School, c. 1930. The Orme Girls' School opened in 1876 in Victoria Road opposite the Boys' High School which opened in the same year. Facing the school is the Crimean Cannon presented to the borough by Samuel Christy MP which stood there between 1857-1965. Although the cannon is now displayed outside the Borough Museum, when it was being transferred some of the girls from the school, fearing that it was to be scrapped, protested and tied a notice to the barrel bearing the message 'Hands off our cannon'.

A tennis match at Orme Girls' School. This action shot, unusual for Edwardian times, shows a tennis match in progress on the courts at the south end of the school, a scene of great gentility and refinement. It is doubtful that Revd Orme would ever have had events such as this in mind when he made his bequest to educate the poor of the town.

Praeposters at Newcastle High School, 1911. These young gentlemen photographed with their headmaster, Mr Harrison, would have been the cream of Newcastle High School's crop, but shortly after this photograph was taken Saunders, Gwynne, Bagguley and Sammy Wilton, (see pp 115 and 121), lost their lives in France during the First World War . Wilton was posthumously awarded the Military Cross; Woolley and Southwell who both survived, also won Military Crosses.

Newcastle High School's speech day, *c.* 1890. This unusual interior photograph shows speech-day in the school hall. The latest readable date on the boards between the windows is 1889, and ladies in the audience are wearing hats which are decidedly Victorian rather than Edwardian. After the First World War, the hall was panelled and known thereafter as the Memorial Hall.

Ici on parle Francais, Newcastle High School, *c.* 1900. 'Here one speaks French'. Another photograph showing the contrast between the large classes at schools such as Friarswood and the select 'boater-wearing' groups at Newcastle High School. Access to such education for the sons and daughters of the professional and business classes clearly helped to maintain the status quo.

Nine

Getting Around

Carriages outside the Globe Commercial Hotel, Red Lion Square, *c.* 1900. Situated on a major north-south, east-west crossroads, Newcastle had been a major coaching town since the eighteenth century. At the height of the coaching era coaches would leave the original Globe Hotel, which this one replaced, for London, Liverpool, Birmingham and Manchester. Although coaching declined after the arrival of the railways, coaches still took people and parcels to and from the station. One of the notices in the hotel window advertises transport to the Golf Links (see p. 28).

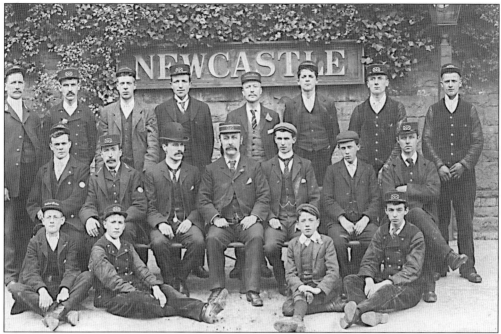

The staff at Newcastle Station, King Street, c. 1900. The stationmaster, possibly William Holbrook, sits in the centre of the picture. The younger boys seated at the front are porters. Most of the staff are wearing caps bearing the Stafford knot and initials NSR for North Staffordshire Railway. Four of the caps read 'Outdoor Porter'.

Newcastle Railway Station, 1964, just before the line was closed in 1965 and the cutting at the Brampton filled in. The photograph clearly shows the location of the station and the line heading towards the goods yard in the distance. The old cuttings are now used as public walks, imaginatively called Station Walks.

A locomotive passing through Liverpool Road Halt in the 1960s. After the First World War this halt was used by rail motors which consisted of only one carriage, hence the short platform. Rail motors, introduced to compete with trams, had a short life and there were only three on the North Staffordshire Railways. The workers at Enderley Mills would use this halt on their way to and from work.

An atmospheric photograph showing the 43026 locomotive shunting at Silverdale Colliery in January 1964. In the background can be seen the winding gear for the mine. In 1850 the line was opened, linking Silverdale to Pool Dam where there was a large coal depot.

Madeley Road Station, *c.* 1927. The stationmaster at this time was Mr Dan Massey. This line linked Newcastle and Market Drayton and was opened in 1870. It was closed to passenger services in 1956. The photographer was Augusta M. Taverner.

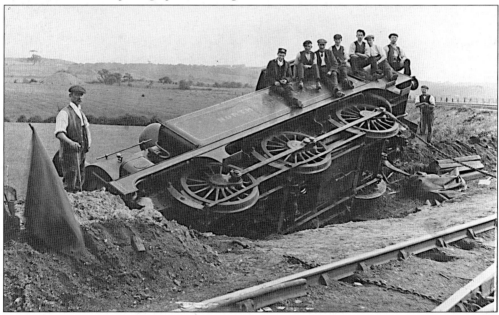

A derailment of a North Staffordshire Railway locomotive on the Audley line, 1912. The train guard sits on the tender whilst the other men would have been called out to dig out the locomotive and are awaiting the arrival of the steam crane to set it back on the rails. The postcard is stamped 1912.

Two train tickets issued on the Silverdale to Newcastle line in the 1960s.

Smith and Sons 'Taxi' service outside J. Dean the cloggers at Butt Lane around the 1920s. According to a trade directory of 1932, Smith and Sons obviously did not like 'putting all their eggs in one basket' and consequently were simultaneously in business as grocers and undertakers and also owned a motor garage in Kidsgrove.

Coaches parked near Audley Station, *c.* 1920. An increase in public transport and coach companies made travel easier so people's horizons were broadened. This fleet of coaches is probably about to set off taking Audley residents for a day trip.

A charabanc belonging to the Motor Coach & Service Company, Wolstanton, *c.* 1920.

A limousine built by Henry Farr Ltd of Brunswick Street, Newcastle, c. 1924. Farr's were established in 1830 as carriage builders. Rather than go out of business when the market for horse-drawn vehicles was waning, Farrs, unlike many other companies changed with the times and started building motor cars instead.

An advertisement from a directory of 1854 for the company of Henry Farr & Son Ltd.

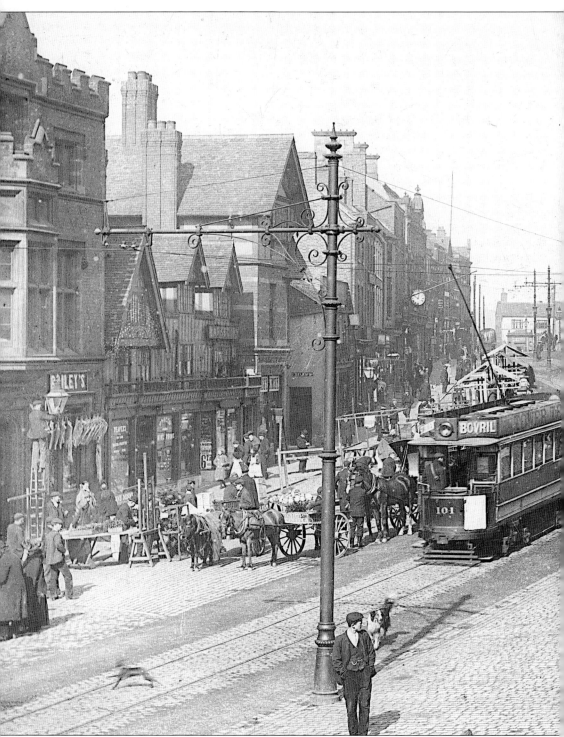

Newcastle High Street, *c.* 1911. This busy shot shows the townspeople going about their everyday business and shows the path taken by the tram lines up from Red Lion Square. Trams were introduced to the town at the turn of the twentieth century, and ran from Newcastle to

Chesterton, Silverdale, Hanley, Wolstanton and Burslem. Tram services were withdrawn in 1928 being superseded by bus services. In the market, farmers would sell their wares from carts – the usual form of transport used to reach the market! (The William Colville Collection)

J.T. Stubbs' delivery van decorated for what appears to be a banana promotion! Stubbs' was a fruit merchant of Kidsgrove. The children sitting on the van have had their faces blacked out, not very politically correct, and each is holding a bunch of bananas. The gentleman on the far left is probably Mr Stubbs himself.

Congestion on the High Street looking south, *c.* 1960. With an increase in the use of motor vehicles, the volume of traffic through the medieval streets of Newcastle took its toll as can be seen in this photograph. The new ring road around the centre was constructed in the 1960s to ease the pressure of traffic. This ring road dramatically altered the appearance of the town.

Ten
Days to Remember

Opening of the Municipal Hall, 1890. A parade, passing by St John's church, Liverpool Road, including the Lord Mayor of London, wends its way to the official opening of the Municipal Hall. Both the laying of the foundation stone and official opening were important civic occasions, but despite this the building itself was to be demolished less than eighty years after its opening.

Laying the foundation stone of the Ashfields' Wesleyan Mission Sunday School, *c.* 1908. A caption is largely unnecessary for this photograph as the only information missing from the large sign in the photograph is the date. The fashions are clearly Edwardian and as the following photograph reveals that the Sunday School opened in 1909, this photograph must therefore date from around 1908-1909. The only known member of the crowd is William Harold Brown of Brown & Corbishley the solicitors.

Ashfields' Wesleyan Mission Sunday School, 1909. The notice inside the gate identifies the opening of the new Ashfields' Wesleyan Mission (Sunday) School in 1909. Those present at the event clearly span the social strata of the town; some of those pictured appearing quite grand, whilst one poor woman on the left looks drawn and has no hat, a sure sign of her reduced circumstances. William Harold Brown was again present.

Procession at Chesterton, *c.* 1911. This procession in Chesterton was probably photographed on 22 June 1911, the day of the Coronation of King George V and Queen Mary. The royal couple were to visit Newcastle themselves in both 1913 and 1925. The road running left to right along the bottom was presumably the main street, as there are tram-lines set into the cobbles.

King George V and Queen Mary at Birchenwood Colliery, April 1913. The King and Queen visited North Staffordshire on 22 and 23 April 1913. Whilst in the area they visited various pottery factories, Birchenwood Colliery – where this photograph was taken – and also attended a civic reception in Newcastle.

King George & Queen Mary in Newcastle 22 April 1913. This photograph shows the royal couple on the dais in Nelson Place. In front of them, the rather rotund gentleman apparently leading the cheers is Mayor William Mellard, owner of the High Street ironmongery business. Although no longer located in Newcastle, William Mellard & Sons are still in business today as steel stockholders.

King George V and Queen Mary at Newcastle, 5 June 1925. This photograph shows the Royal landau entering Nelson Place from Brunswick Street on 5 June 1925, cheered on by huge crowds. The cinema appears to be presenting *Darwin was Right* probably a discourse on *The Origin of Species*. Charles Darwin himself was a regular visitor to the borough having married Emma Wedgwood, the daughter of Josiah Wedgwood II, at Maer.

Visit of the Prince of Wales to Newcastle, 1925. One of the town's earliest surviving buildings, 'The Star' is shown here decorated with bunting as a welcome to the Prince of Wales. To the right is Hubanks' greengrocers, occupying that part of the inn which had been converted to retail in 1869. The blackboard outside 'The Star' reads 'Visit of HRH The Prince of Wales to Newcastle-under-Lyme'.

This photograph shows the newly chosen Mayor of Newcastle Joseph Griffith, in 1881, and was

y Edwin Harrison.

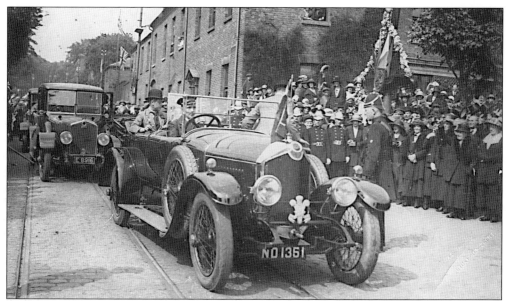

Visit of the Prince of Wales to Newcastle, 1925. Edward, Prince of Wales' motorcade arrives from Queen Street for a civic reception in Nelson Place. Appropriately the dais was positioned in front of the fine Georgian block between King Street and Queen Street. The building in the background, now Brown & Corbishley's solicitors' offices, was the home of Dr F.H. Northen around 1800, and remained a doctor's surgery for a century and a half.

Beating the Bounds at Audley, 1913. Historically, children would be taken to the manor's boundaries and subjected to some sort of physical discomfort, the intention being to firmly fix these boundaries into their memory. In the distant past this would have been a very important lesson, when straying onto a neighbouring Lord's lands might have been punishable by death. Today when carried out this tradition seems simply quaint.

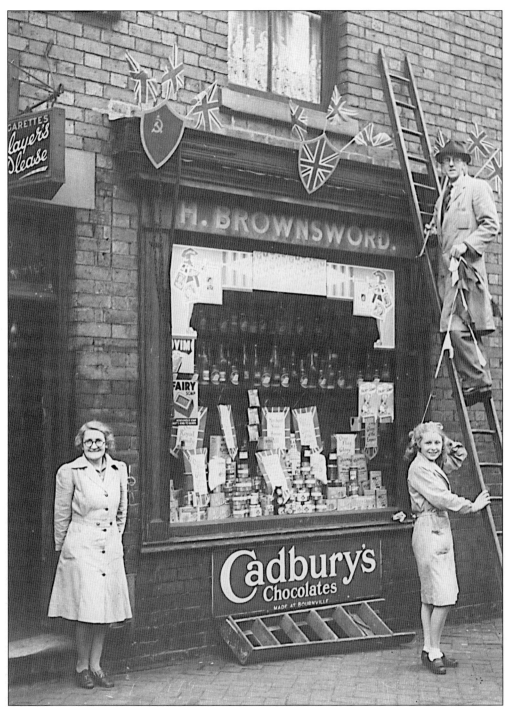

This charming photograph shows the Brownsword family decorating their North Street shop to celebrate the end of the Second World War. Notices bear the patriotic messages 'Merchant Navy, Heroes All' and 'Our Flag, Glory of the Empire'. The appearance of Russian insignia next to those of the UK and US might seem incongruous at first to those who have grown up through the 'Cold War'.

This photograph was taken at the VE Day celebrations May 1945 in Chesterton High Street. The happy group seems to include no adult women, perhaps because they were elsewhere preparing the food. It is likely that rationing necessitated a fairly Spartan repast but on this occasion it was probably relished like champagne and caviar!

Princess Elizabeth, the Mayor, Mayoress and other dignitaries pictured during their tour of Enderley Mills on 2 November 1949. The mill specialised in the manufacture of service uniforms and one of the managing directors of the mill is shown explaining to the visitors what part each machinist played in the process.

Princess Elizabeth in Newcastle, 2 November 1949. A smiling Princess Elizabeth with her RAF Officer escort, Group Captain E.L.S. Ward DFC of Tern Hill, makes her way up the Ironmarket to the Municipal Hall where she was to take tea with the Mayor, Alderman William Evanson, Mrs Evanson and their guests.

Mayor-choosing, 1890s. Each year from the 1860s Newcastle's dignitaries, and anyone else who wanted to, would converge on the Market Cross to be photographed with the newly chosen mayor. These images provide fascinating insights into such things as fashions, changes in uniforms, shop-

owners and their wares, as well as providing a visual record of the mayors themselves. In this fascinating view a Scottish piper can be seen on the carriage in the background; was this because the new mayor was a Scot or was the Duke of Sutherland perhaps present?

The visit of Queen Elizabeth and Prince Philip to Newcastle, 25 May 1973. The Queen and Prince Philip pause during their walkabout in the High Street and exchange words with the Mayor, Councillor Reginald Lane and his deputy, Councillor Charles Mitchell.

Her Majesty the Queen meets some of her younger subjects during a walkabout in High Street during her visit on 25 May 1973. The royal visit was part of the celebrations to commemorate the 800th anniversary of the granting of the charter giving the town borough status.

Eleven
Kith and Kin

The Wiltons had a profound effect on Newcastle as builders, but it is the branch of the family concerned with butchery who are probably better remembered today. Samuel (on the left) built May Bank School, the King Edward VII Memorial Baths and many other local buildings. His son 'Sammy', is seated on his grandfather Samuel's knee, (see p. 89).

Sadly the bride and groom in this Edwardian wedding group are unknown and only two of the guests are known, Thomas and 'Cissie' Beasley. Both Thomas and his wife appear on the following photograph.

A rare opportunity to see inside an ordinary Edwardian home. The occasion is the 'wedding breakfast' of the couple at the head of the table. The photograph was probably only made possible by the large windows and white tablecloth acting as a reflector. The image gives a useful insight into home furnishing of the period, complete with aspidistra and horn gramophone.

This elderly gentleman and two young girls, probably his granddaughters, are members of the Brownsword family (see p. 109).

(see p. 109)

This Harrison portrait shows Mrs Ann Berks Smith on her one hundred and second birthday. An earlier Harrison portrait shows her on her one hundreth birthday.

Mellard/Mosley wedding party at The Firs, 12 August 1891. 'The Firs', now better known as Newcastle Borough Museum and Art Gallery can be seen behind the wedding guests at the marriage of Richard Bartlett Mellard and Beatrice Mosley whose family occupied the house.

The Mellards were the Ironmongers of High Street and the Mosleys ran a drapery business also in High Street. Both Richard Bartlett and his father William front row (third from left) were mayors of the town, Richard Bartlett on four occasions.

This family picture shows three generations of the Boyce-Adams family, last private residents of 'The Firs' before it was purchased by Newcastle Borough Council and became the Borough Museum and Art Gallery. The family ran high-class grocery establishments in Ironmarket, Newcastle and Piccadilly, Hanley. Robert Boyce-Adams, the baby in the photograph, still lives nearby on land retained by the family at the time of the sale.

The Caddick Adams family's nanny dressed as Queen Victoria for an unknown event.

Samuel Wilton, 1892-1917. S.B. Wilton photographed in uniform at the family's builder's yard, Newcastle. 'Sammy' Wilton was a pupil at Newcastle High School and from there went up to Cambridge. After graduating he volunteered for the army and fought in France in the First World War where he was wounded on three separate occasions, the last time fatally. For his bravery he was mentioned in despatches and posthumously awarded the Military Cross. In this photograph he appears to be recuperating from one of his wounds and is leaning on a stick (see p. 89).

This unusual and sad 'family photograph' shows Sammy Wilton's grave in France. The inscription reads: 'In loving Memory of Capt. S.B. Wilton M.C. 5th North Staffordshire Regiment of Newcastle-under-Lyme Who fell in action March 14th 1917 Aged 24 years. Kindly he lived and Bravely he died.' Sammy was the last in a line of Samuel Wiltons, builders and burgesses of Newcastle, stretching back to at least 1798.

This Parton portrait shows Jesse Augustus Bailey who was born on 10 April 1897.

The Burgess family of May Bank, 1940. This family picture taken by Harry Burgess shows Private Stan Burgess in his new uniform with his younger brothers Graham, Frank and Alan. The photograph was taken at Highfield Avenue May Bank, and behind the group can be seen some of the appalling air pollution which used to be present in the valley separating Newcastle from Hanley.

Twelve
Religion and Religious Buildings

St Giles' church pre-1873. This Edwin Harrison photograph shows the exterior of Newcastle Parish church prior to its demolition in 1873. The Georgian church was built in 1725 after its predecessor was damaged by fire. This had been started deliberately by members of the St Giles' congregation, intent on burning down the adjacent non-conformist meeting house, but the fire eventually rendered both places of worship unusable.

Interior of St Giles' church by Harrison, pre-1873. This photograph shows the interior of the apse of the Georgian church demolished in 1873. The definition of the print is so good that much of the Ten Commandments on either side of the altar can be read together with every word of the Memorial to the Revd Clement Leigh, former rector of the church, who died in 1853.

This photograph shows the view from the apse towards the organ loft of the Georgian church. In the foreground can be seen the top of the font cover, and on the left the beautifully modelled wrought iron mace-stand which today forms part of the metalwork collection at the Victoria and Albert Museum.

The pre-1873 St Giles' church from Red Lion Square.

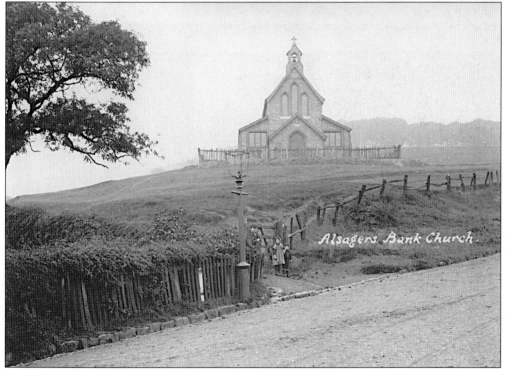

A view of the newly-built Alsagers Bank church, around 1911, standing like a beacon on what appears at the time to have been heathland. Behind and to the left is the end of the Apedale Valley. This scene appears very different today.

An excellent picture postcard of the church of St Peter's at Maer, postmarked 16 May 1906. Coincidentally this card was sent to (Olive) May Wilton of 5 Merrial Street, Newcastle who appears in the photograph on p. 115 with the rest of her family, including her nephew 'Sammy'.

Chesterton Congregational Sunday School Parade. This postcard is probably a rare item, with only a few copies produced, showing a Chesterton Congregational Sunday School Parade. The location is easily identifiable as Broadmeadows because postcards exist of the same scene without the procession. The street furniture and rails show that it was taken after the arrival of trams in Chesterton. It can be seen that trams did traverse rural areas and were not only a feature of town centres.

Audley Wesleyan Methodist church. Audley has traditionally had a high percentage of Protestant nonconformists, a more common factor in urban areas than rural ones, except in the north of the county. The presence of a large congregation of Wesleyan Methodists in villages like Audley has been connected to the presence of iron-workings and coal-mining.

The Ebenezer Chapel in Marsh Street was built in 1858 to replace an earlier chapel. With its congregation falling the chapel was closed and sold in the late 1970s, a new chapel being built behind the Lecture Rooms in Merrial Street. The old chapel was renamed Ebenezer House and opened as a department store, now occupied by an accountancy firm. Part of the beautifully carved oak staircase salvaged from Maer Hall was installed by the proprietors at the time. (The William Colville Collection)

The Revd Albert Baines, vicar of St George's church, 1905-1910, (2nd row, 6th from left), amongst a large group of men, including other clergymen. Revd Baines' efforts largely concentrated on increasing the number of men in his congregation and to this end he founded a number of societies concentrating on male pursuits, (see p. 81).

St Peter's Mission, Friarswood Road. The corrugated iron and timber St Peter's Mission was originally used as a place of worship; it opened in 1890, and served its congregation for fifty years. Later as pupil numbers at the adjacent Friarswood School rose, it served as a classroom and finally as a scout hut before being burnt down in an arson attack in the 1970s.